T0208771

BE YOU BEYOUTIFUL

3 MINUTE DEVOTIONS

31 DAY DEVOTIONAL FOR TEEN GIRLS

CHASITY N. DOUYON

authorHOUSE®

AuthorHouse™
1663 Liberty Drive
Bloomington, IN 47403
www.authorhouse.com
Phone: 1 (800) 839-8640

Published by AuthorHouse 6/20/2020

ISBN: 978-1-7283-6543-5 (sc)
ISBN: 978-1-7283-6542-8 (e)

Print information available on the last page.

Be You
BeYOUtiful
3 Minute Devotional for Teen Girls
31 Days
By Chasity N. Douyon

I'd like to dedicate this book to some
very special young ladies:
Jaycee D.; Ellayna H., Olivia H., Eva H.,
Sophia H., Shelton C., Mary Michelle C.
Sadie K., Natalie G., Savannah B.
Emily P., Elizabeth B., and Jules C.

<u>Day 1</u>

1 Timothy 4:12 King James Version (KJV)

Let no man despise thy youth; but be thou an example of the believers, in word, in conversation, in charity, in spirit, in faith, in purity.

Have you ever felt you were too young to make a difference? Well, I can tell you that, that is a lie from the enemy. God's Word tells us to not let others look down on us because we are young. God says we can be an example for other believers at a young age. As a teen, I didn't feel that I could truly make a difference. I honestly just tried my best to live for God and to not give in to the pressures of society. I grew up in church and loved going to church with my family. God used me to be a witness to my friends and they would ask me for advice and for prayer because they knew I was a believer. You can truly make a difference in the life of those around you. If you come from a family where you are the only believer, continue to pursue Christ. You could be the one to help draw your family into the family of God.

Reflection

1. What are some ways you can make a difference at your age?

2. Who has been an example for you in your life?

Chasity N. Douyon

Day 2

Romans 10:9-10 King James Version (KJV)

That if thou shalt confess with thy mouth the Lord Jesus, and shalt believe in thine heart that God hath raised him from the dead, thou shalt be saved.

For with the heart, man believeth unto righteousness; and with the mouth confession is made unto salvation.

Have you received Jesus Christ as your Lord and Savior? He is waiting to embrace you with open arms. He loves you with an everlasting love and always has loved you. He wants you to live with Him throughout eternity. He wants you to trust Him with your heart and your life. He wants you to know that you do not have to do anything to receive His love because it's already yours. Do you feel like you're not good enough to come to Jesus? Jesus doesn't think you're not good enough; He calls you more than enough. If you want to accept Him as your Lord and Savior all you have to do is believe in your heart and confess with your mouth that Jesus Christ is Lord and was raised from the dead. Now you are saved. Welcome to the family of God! I am so glad to have you as a new sister in Christ!

Reflection

1. How did you feel when you first accepted Jesus into your heart?

2. Is there someone you can tell about Jesus so that they may come to know Him as well?

Chasity N. Douyon

Day 3

Proverbs 29:25 King James Version (KJV)

The fear of man bringeth a snare: but whoso putteth his trust in the Lord shall be safe.

Have you ever worried about what others think about you? I have. I used to be crippled by fear of what others thought about me. It hasn't been until recent years that I have gained freedom in this area by the grace of God. Don't be afraid to be different. Don't be afraid to not do all the things your friends do. If your parents do not feel comfortable with you hanging out with certain friends or going to certain places, trust them. Your parents love you and have lived in your shoes before where they wanted to hang out with friends who may not have been good influences. They already know how things could end up and they do not want that for you. I used to think I was missing out on so much because my mother was strict and did not let me hang out with all of my friends from school. But I learned that she was right because I wouldn't have felt comfortable going to some of the places they went to. I realized for myself that some of the friends I had were not ones that were good influences and I really didn't want to do what they did. I never really fit in, but I realized why later in life: I was born to stand out.

Reflection

1. Have you ever felt like you had to gain the approval of others to fit in?

2. How do you overcome worrying about what others think about you?

Chasity N. Douyon

Day 4

Deuteronomy 31:8 King James Version (KJV)

And the Lord, he it is that doth go before thee; he will be with thee, he will not fail thee, neither forsake thee: fear not, neither be dismayed.

Have you ever been really sad and felt alone? I felt intense sadness and loneliness after I lost my dad at the age of 13. I couldn't wrap my mind around not getting to see him again. Not having him walk me down the aisle someday or watch me graduate. At a young age, I learned to find comfort in the fact that I have a Heavenly Father who will never leave me. He was with me in my sad and lonely moments. He reminded me that He would always look out for me and protect me. You may not have a good relationship with your earthly father, but know that your Heavenly Father loves you and cares for you always. There is nothing you can do to lose His love or earn His love, it is already yours.

Reflection:

1. What do you do when you feel sad and alone?

2. What are some positive things you can do when you feel sad to help you feel better?

Day 5

Philippians 4:6-8 King James Version (KJV)

Be careful for nothing; but in every thing by prayer and supplication with thanksgiving let your requests be made known unto God.

And the peace of God, which passeth all understanding, shall keep your hearts and minds through Christ Jesus.

Have you ever been anxious about something? Maybe you had a big test coming up that you didn't feel confident about or you had to do a speech for class and public speaking makes your palms all sweaty. You can pray and ask God to help you in those moments you feel anxious. I have and still deal with anxiety from time to time. I have learned that the times I feel the most anxious are when I'm trying to do things in my own power. I have also learned that each time I ask God into my anxious situation, He shows up and brings peace with Him. His word tells us that He will do this for us when we come to Him in prayer. Know that your anxiety is not God's will for your life; He wants you to lean on Him and trust in Him. He wants to exchange your anxious thoughts for His perfect peace.

Reflection:

1. Think about a time when you felt anxious. What did you do to help ease your anxiety?

2. Have you ever experienced a time when you felt God's peace in an overwhelming way?

Day 6

1 Thessalonians 5:11 King James Version (KJV)

Wherefore comfort yourselves together, and edify one another, even as also ye do.

Have you ever been bullied? I have and it's not a fun feeling at all. God calls us to encourage one another and build each other up, not tear each other down. Even if all of your classmates are doing it, you can be the one who chooses to show kindness to the one who is being bullied. You never know the impact it can have on that person. Put yourself in the other person's shoes and imagine it was you being belittled, ridiculed, made fun of. How would this make you feel? Or if you have been the one who has been made fun of before, you can remember how it made you feel. You don't want to be the reason someone else feels that way, so choose to be kind.

Reflection:

1. Do you have friends who encourage you?

2. What can you do when you see someone else getting bullied?

Day 7

Zephaniah 3:17 King James Version (KJV)

The Lord thy God in the midst of thee is mighty; he will save, he will rejoice over thee with joy; he will rest in his love, he will joy over thee with singing.

This verse has always been so captivating to me. God rejoices over us with singing. He takes great delight in us. This reminds me that God is proud of me. Have you ever felt your heart swell when someone told you they were proud of you? I sure have. When you have worked hard at something and accomplish it and someone else recognizes your accomplishment it feels good. You may be on the other end of this feeling and may not have people around you who tell you they are proud of you or celebrate you when you do well. You can rest assured that when you make that good decision, you complete that task, you do that good deed, that your Heavenly Father is proud of you. He rejoices over you with singing. Imagine Him singing "I'm so proud of you. I love you with an everlasting love. I'm so glad you're mine." I don't know about you but this makes me happy just thinking about it.

Reflection:

1. How do you feel when someone says they are proud
   of you?

2. Think about your favorite artist singing your favorite
   song. God's song over you is even more beautiful than
   that.

Day 8

Esther 4:14 King James Version (KJV)

14 For if thou altogether holdest thy peace at this time, then shall there enlargement and deliverance arise to the Jews from another place; but thou and thy father's house shall be destroyed: and who knoweth whether thou art come to the kingdom for such a time as this?

Esther is my favorite book of the Bible. I mean how cool is it that she saved an entire group of people, God's people, by doing something that was very scary to her? It could have cost her, her life but she did it anyway knowing that she had the power of the Almighty God behind her. I'd like to say to never be afraid to challenge yourself. I found myself given the opportunity to influence people who were older than me even, because of doors God opened for me to walk through. You may be asked to be in a leadership position in a club at school and may be wondering why someone would ask you to do this. It could be so that you can bring about positive change in your school or in the lives of others. God may have you in that position for such a time as this.

Reflection:

1. Think about a time when you successfully did something you were afraid to do. How did you feel after you accomplished it?

2. What are some things you can do to positively influence those around you?

Day 9

Proverbs 12:26 King James Version (KJV)

The righteous is more excellent than his neighbour: but the way of the wicked seduceth them.

Have you ever been betrayed by a friend? I have had several friends who have turned their backs on me. Funny thing is that before it happened I was always shown that they weren't a true friend. These kinds of friends would try to take advantage of my friendship. They would use me and then would leave to live their life when I needed them. It wasn't until sometime after they were gone that I realized I was better off. Anytime God allowed someone to leave my life, He always brought more people in. I can honestly say the friends I have now are true friends who love me and support me. Be mindful of the friends you have. Do not let others use you and never reciprocate friendship. If we do things, yes, we do them from the good of our hearts. But we should have friends who do things for us sometimes as well; friends who show us that they care and don't make the friendship feel one-sided.

Reflection:

1. Have you ever had a friendship that felt one-sided? How did that make you feel?

2. Have you ever had a friend tell you that they felt your friendship was one-sided? How did that make you feel?

Day 10

Proverbs 27:17 King James Version (KJV)

[17] Iron sharpeneth iron; so a man sharpeneth the countenance of his friend.

Your friends should help you become a better you. They will call you out when you are doing wrong or not living up to your potential. Keep these friends close to your heart. As a matter of fact, my friends encourage me and prayed for me as I wrote this devotional. They reminded me that God has great plans for me and that I'm capable of doing great things. Your friends can remind you of your worth and value, even when you do not feel it yourself. Knowing that your friends love and support you is such a great feeling. Your friends should not tear you down, they should build you up. Friends can help push us to our greatest potential.

Reflection:

1. Do the friends you have now encourage you to do good things or bad things?

2. Are you the type of friend that encourages your friends?

Day 11

Romans 8:38-39 King James Version (KJV)

For I am persuaded, that neither death, nor life, nor angels, nor principalities, nor powers, nor things present, nor things to come,

Nor height, nor depth, nor any other creature, shall be able to separate us from the love of God, which is in Christ Jesus our Lord.

Have you ever made a big mistake? Maybe one that caused you to feel shame or feel embarrassed even. Have you ever gone to your parents about the mistake and had them acknowledge that you made a mistake but it did not change their love for you? Sweet girl, this is only a glimpse of what our Father's unconditional love is like for you. There is nothing you can do to make Him love you any less or to withdraw His love from you. His love is a gift you have for life. Even when you don't choose to receive it, it's still yours. Even when you choose to not follow Him, He still loves you. He longs to have a relationship with you and for you to feel His love everyday of your life. Remember that God loves you!

Reflection:

1. Have you ever felt like God didn't love you?

2. Has someone ever told you that they didn't love you? How did that make you feel?

__Day 12__

Micah 7:19 King James Version (KJV)

He will turn again, he will have compassion upon us; he will subdue our iniquities, and thou wilt cast all their sins into the depths of the sea.

When you make mistakes you can come to God and ask for forgiveness with a sincere heart and He forgives you. As we see in the scripture, He tosses our sin into the depths of the sea. Some scholars have referred to this as the "Sea of Forgetfulness" meaning God no longer keeps a record of it. When I find myself being bothered by previous sins that I have been forgiven of, I think about how God doesn't remember it. It's like I can be like "God, remember that one time I did such and such?" And God's response would be no because it is forgiven and blotted out. How amazing is it to think about that?! So the next time the enemy comes to you with old news, you can remind him that God has forgiven you and no longer remembers your forgiven sin. That you are walking in God's freedom and forgiveness.

Reflection:

1. Is it hard for you to forgive others?

2. Do you find it hard to forgive yourself?

Day 13

Isaiah 28:23 King James Version (KJV)

Give ye ear, and hear my voice; hearken, and hear my speech.

Have you ever felt like God told you to do something? How did you know God "spoke" to you? This verse mentions the words "voice" and "speech." There are some people who say they have audibly heard God's voice. This is one way God can speak to us to catch our attention. But God also speaks to us through His Word. He can place it on your heart to read a certain scripture and it ends up being just what you need to see for your current situation. God has done this for me before time and time again. I have also prayed for friends and He has given me scriptures to send to them which ended up being something they needed to hear. It is so important that we listen to God. After we pray we need to take time to listen to God and hear what He wants to say to us. I heard Pastor Michael Todd mention talking to God and it being like talking to a friend and venting to them and then hanging up the phone. We didn't give them time to respond to us. Think about this the next time you pray, be sure to take time to listen.

Reflection:

1. Have you ever had someone hang up the phone while you were trying to tell them something? How did that make you feel?

2. Is there something you feel like God has told you to do?

Day 14

Psalm 86:9-10 King James Version (KJV)

All nations whom thou hast made shall come and worship before thee, O Lord; and shall glorify thy name.

For thou art great, and doest wondrous things: thou art God alone.

I don't know about you but I LOVE worship! You don't have to be a good singer or be able to keep up with a beat to worship God. I don't have the best singing voice but when I feel God's presence during worship I don't care what I sound like, I just want to worship my God. There are several ways to worship God other than just singing, you can also worship God in your giving, the work you do, and with your life. God loves it when we worship Him; Psalm 22:3 tells us that "God inhabits the praises of His people." When we worship God we are giving him the glory that He deserves. We don't just worship Him for what He does or has done; we worship Him for who He is. We should love to worship God and we can rest assured that He is near when we worship Him.

Reflection:

1. What is your favorite worship song?

2. How do you feel when you worship God?

Day 15

1 Peter 5:6-7 King James Version (KJV)

Humble yourselves therefore under the mighty hand of God, that he may exalt you in due time:

Casting all your care upon him; for he careth for you.

Have you ever felt so weighed down with anxiety about something? I sure have. It could be telling someone something really hard, a thing I needed to do but was afraid to do, or even sometimes just being nervous about talking to others because I tend to be shy. The word cast here means to "throw off." If we think about this in terms of fishing and casting a net, as is often referenced in regards to this verse, we can think of it as getting the net out of the boat so that we can catch hold of something with the net. We can think of anxiety like a net because we often feel so entangled in it. But when we cast it off of us, we can catch hold to something else; God's peace. God really does care about you and does not want you to live in a constant state of anxiety.

Reflection:

1. Have you ever asked God to take away your anxiety in a moment you were feeling anxious?

2. Do you feel like God cares for you?

Day 16

Matthew 22:39 King James Version (KJV)

And the second is like unto it, Thou shalt love thy neighbour as thyself.

This verse tells us God's second greatest commandment. That is that we love one another as we love ourselves. First, we must love ourselves. God created you in His image; you are a reflection of God. You may not like all of the things about you, your weird ways, the big glasses you have to wear in order to see, or even your voice, but you should love yourself. With this same love, you should love your neighbor. Yes, that means your neighbor who doesn't look like you, who doesn't have the same beliefs as you, who don't have as much money as your family has. We should not carry prejudice in our heart towards our neighbor. You should show love to all because all are God's creations. We all bleed the same blood and are able to be saved by the same God.

Reflection:

1. Do you have hate in your heart towards a person, a certain race, a certain group of kids at school? Pray and ask God to replace the hate with love for those people.

2. Do you love yourself?

Chasity N. Douyon

Day 17

Philippians 4:13 King James Version (KJV)

I can do all things through Christ which strengtheneth me.

Have you ever felt like you couldn't do something? I had a friend who played tennis and was nervous about a match she had coming up. I went to her tennis match along with a sign I made with this verse on it. I held the sign up during her match so she could look at it when she needed to. This verse is a great reminder that there is nothing you can't do with the help of God. I have often quoted this verse before having to get up and speak in front of a group of people. I have also quoted this verse when I conquered a fear, like my first time riding a jet ski. This verse can be used to encourage yourself and those around you when someone has to face a fear or do something they feel is hard.

Reflection:

1. Can you think of a time that you quoted this verse over yourself?

2. What was the outcome of what you had to go through?

Day 18

1 Timothy 6:10 King James Version (KJV)

For the love of money is the root of all evil: which while some coveted after, they have erred from the faith, and pierced themselves through with many sorrows.

Have you ever dreamed of being rich? I think at one point we all have. There is nothing wrong with having money. However, there is a problem when you have a love for money. The love of money is what can cause a person to cheat others out of money because they just want more for themselves. There are many stories about people with great wealth who are alone because they loved obtaining money more than they did other areas of their lives. There are those who have worked long hours to continue to have a lot of money and in turn, it cost them their family. Don't let the love of money enter your heart. It is nice to have money, but do not let it cost you your family, your friendships, or even your life.

Reflection

1. How can you use your money wisely and be a blessing to others?

2. Can you think of a story of someone who had great wealth but lost friends, family, or their life over money?

Day 19

Psalm 119:105 King James Version (KJV)

Thy word is a lamp unto my feet, and a light unto my path.

We can use God's word to guide us when we have to make decisions. God's word is filled with answers for many different kinds of scenarios that we may face. When I have to make big decisions I like to pray and ask God for guidance. He typically always gives me a scripture to read and it points me in the right direction. These big decisions can range from making a big purchase, deciding which college to attend, or deciding to try a new small group at church. God's word can illuminate the path before us so that we can clearly see what it is that God wants us to do. You don't have to stumble in the dark; you can go to the Word of God and ask for guidance.

Reflection

1. Have you ever used God's word to help you make a big decision?

2. Have you ever had a friend who has had to make a big decision and God gave you a scripture to tell them?

Day 20

Exodus 20:12 King James Version (KJV)

Honour thy father and thy mother: that thy days may be long upon the land which the Lord thy God giveth thee.

The Bible tells us that it is important to honor our parents. God gave us parents to help give us earthly guidance throughout our life. You honor your parents by doing what they ask you to, by respecting them and loving them. My mother used to always tell my brother and me that we were "shortening our days" when we didn't follow her instructions. As a young child, this made me think twice about not listening to her because I wanted to live a long life. My mother was very strict as I was growing up and at times I resented it. Looking back, I realize that she was trying to protect me from things the best way she felt she could. God made your parents, your parents for a reason. God knew the personality you would have and how your parents would be able to raise you to follow Him. Sadly, if your parents are abusive, please know that this is not God's will for how they should be. You can honor your parents by praying for God to change their hearts.

Reflection:

1. Think about how God feels when we disobey Him. How do you think your parents feel when you disobey them?

2. Have you told your parents that you love them lately?

Chasity N. Douyon

Day 21

Hebrews 13:1 King James Version (KJV)

Let brotherly love continue.

Do you have a sibling? My parents both came from large families. My mom had 9 siblings and my dad had 16! I can't even imagine how it must have been for them, but I have heard some stories. I grew up with an older brother and I can attest to how rough that can be at times. We used to argue and fight a lot. I didn't like him telling me what to do and he didn't like that he felt like I was "babied." There were many times I wished I was an only child. But as we have grown older, we have learned how to get along better. We still have our moments but that comes with having a sibling. I do know one thing though, I wouldn't let anyone be mean to him or try to harm him. This is the same love we should have for all because we are brothers and sisters in Christ. This means there may be people who we don't always get along with, but we should love them.

Reflection

1. How would you feel if someone was mean to your sibling? If you're an only child, think of how you would feel if someone was mean to your best friend.

2. Can you think of ways to be nicer to your siblings or your best friend?

Chasity N. Douyon

Day 22

2 Corinthians 12:8-9 King James Version (KJV)

For this thing I besought the Lord thrice, that it might depart from me.

And he said unto me, My grace is sufficient for thee: for my strength is made perfect in weakness. Most gladly, therefore, will I rather glory in my infirmities, that the power of Christ may rest upon me.

Sometimes God says no. When God says no it is not that he is being mean to us or doesn't want us to have good things. When God says no He could be trying to build us in a certain area or it could be for our own protection. God sees what we don't see and He knows how we could be affected by receiving what we want. When you are waiting for an answer and God says no, it can sting a bit at times. You may wonder why He won't answer. But God could be trying to show His strength through you. If we always got everything we wanted, we would never have to lean and depend on God, right? But when we lean on Him we can rest assured that He will give us what we need. When you feel weak, you can ask God to help strengthen you.

Reflection:

1. Has God ever told you no about something you had prayed about?

2. Looking back did you realize that His no was protecting you or an opportunity that He showed His strength in your weakness?

Day 23

2 Corinthians 6 King James Version (KJV)

Be ye not unequally yoked together with unbelievers: for what fellowship hath righteousness with unrighteousness? and what communion hath light with darkness?

We have all been attracted to the "bad boy" at one point in time I'm sure. God tells us to not be yoked together with unbelievers. God's will is for you to be with a guy who loves God more than he loves you. A guy who puts Christ first will know how to treat God's daughter. This is not to say that things will always be sunshine and rainbows because you both still live in a human flesh that wars against the spiritual world. But a guy cannot truly know love unless he knows Christ for Christ IS love. So, if your dating options seem slim, that's ok. Don't settle for someone who mistreats you or does not value the daughter of God that you are. Wait for the one who loves God so that he can properly love you.

Reflections

1. Have you ever dated an unbeliever? Did the relationship seem like a struggle?

2. What are signs you can look for to know if a guy is a follower of Christ?

Day 24

2 Corinthians 6 King James Version (KJV)

And will be a Father unto you, and ye shall be my sons and daughters, saith the Lord Almighty.

Have you lost a parent or both parents? I lost my father when I was 13 years old to murder. It was sudden and very shocking. Sometimes I still don't feel like my dad is dead. It is sad to think about the things he has missed in my life already and that he will miss everything else. But those of us who have lost a parent can rest assured that we have a Heavenly Father who will never leave us. We can go to him with our questions, problems, and happy moments. He watches out for us and protects us. God also makes sure that we have what we need. According to His word, He supplies all of our needs.

Reflection

1. What do you think of when you think of God as your heavenly Father?

2. What are some of your favorite things to do with your dad?

Day 25

Hebrews 11:1 King James Version (KJV)

Now faith is the substance of things hoped for, the evidence of things not seen.

Have you ever prayed for something until you saw it happen? You are exercising your faith. Faith is when we believe and hope for those things that we do not see until we do see them. It takes faith to believe that we have a heavenly Father above. We have not seen Him physically but we can be confident and place assurance in that He is real. One of the biggest moments I can remember when I exercised my faith was when I was a teenager and wanted a car. Now, this did not happen while I was a teenager but I kept believing and having faith that I would get one. My family was not able to purchase a car for me and even with me working; I wasn't able to afford one. I remember praying and believing for a car to be given to me. Big dreams, huh? Well, I was attending a church while I was in college and they actually purchased my first car for me. I remember the day I was presented with my car I sang a song called "He's Able" when they opened the doors with my car sitting out front. Of course, I was overwhelmed with emotions and gratitude. I had faith to believe that God would do what He said he would do and He did! If you're believing for something, hold on to it. God is able to do it for you too!

Reflection

1. What is something you have been praying about? Do you believe it can happen?

2. Is there a person you have been praying to change for the better for some time now? Keep praying and believing.

Chasity N. Douyon

Day 26

But he was wounded for our transgressions, he was bruised for our iniquities: the chastisement of our peace was upon him; and with his stripes we are healed.

Have you ever been really, really sick? The Bible tells us that Jesus took stripes for our healing. I have seen and heard about some miraculous healings in my day. I have seen people be healed from cancer, from diabetes, from migraines. When we are sick we can ask God to come heal us. We can pray for those who are sick and see them be healed. There are times that people receive the ultimate healing and that is to depart from this world and their pain. Yes, it is sad but they are no longer experiencing the pain and anguish of their illness. We have assurance from Christ that if they were a believer that one day they will have a new glorified body. One with no more aches and pains.

Reflection:

1. Have you ever witnessed or heard about someone being healed?

2. Have you been healed of an illness?

Day 27

1 Timothy 2:9-10 King James Version (KJV)

In like manner also, that women adorn themselves in modest apparel, with shamefacedness and sobriety; not with broided hair, or gold, or pearls, or costly array;

But (which becometh women professing godliness) with good works.

I maintained my purity throughout my teen years and am still a virgin until this day. I did not do this in my own strength but through the strength of Christ living in me. Please never feel like you have to show off parts of your body for a young man to like you. A real young man will love your heart and love for the Father more than he loves your appearance. I was never one for keeping up with trends in fashion, not that this is a bad thing because there are some tasteful fashion trends out there today, but it is ok to be different. You don't have to follow the standard, you can set the standard. My prayer for you is that you will be able to maintain your purity until marriage as sex is a beautiful covenant between man and wife according to scripture. I have maintained my purity until this day, even at the age of 28, and I can say it was only due to God protecting me.

God will protect you in your purity if you ask Him to. If you happen to not wait, know that there is grace for you. That you can recommit yourself to purity and that you are not damaged goods. Your Father above still loves you and is still chasing after you.

Reflection:

1. Have you ever felt like you didn't fit in because of the way you dress?

2. What does it mean to you to dress modestly?

Day 28

Mark 1:15 King James Version (KJV)

And saying, The time is fulfilled, and the kingdom of God is at hand: repent ye, and believe the gospel.

Heaven and hell are real. When Jesus died on the cross, He died so that we would be saved from an eternal hell. Yes, Jesus loved you so much that He died for you so that you wouldn't have to experience eternal death. If you're like me, you have heard all of your life that Jesus is coming back soon. Well, I'm here to tell you that this is so true. We can tell by the things that are going on in the world. Jesus can come back at any time because no one knows the day nor the hour when He will return. But we do know that He is coming back because He told us that He was. He went to prepare a place for us where we can live with him forever, heaven. Heaven is more beautiful than the most beautiful sight we have ever seen here on earth. If you want to live with Jesus in heaven, you will need to repent of your sins, believe in Him, and confess with your mouth that Jesus is Lord.

Reflection

1. Have you ever thought about what heaven will look like one day?

2. Do you want to live with Jesus forever?

Chasity N. Douyon

Day 29

Ephesians 4:26 King James Version (KJV)

Be ye angry, and sin not: let not the sun go down upon your wrath:

Have you ever been really angry? I sure have. It is ok to feel angry. You just can't let this anger drive you to sin. Even Jesus felt anger; we see this in Mark 3:5 when Jesus healed the man with the withered hand. He was angry with those in the synagogue for having hardened hearts. We do not want to let the sun go down on our wrath because we never know when it will be our last day or the last day of the person we are angry with. Before my dad got killed he was very upset with me. We had not talked in two weeks because he was so mad he wouldn't talk to me. The morning of the day he got killed I answered the phone when he called and he talked to me for a while before asking to speak with my mother. I cherish that memory now and am so glad to know he didn't die upset with me nor me with him. Don't take it for granted that you have the opportunity to make things right with someone.

Reflection

1. What are some things you can do when you're angry to help yourself calm down?

2. Try to make things right with those you love if you have anger in your heart towards them.

Day 30

Genesis 1:1 King James Version (KJV)

In the beginning God created the heaven and the earth.

One of my favorite things about God's creation is seeing beautiful sunsets at the end of the day. God created many beautiful things when He created the world. He created the world by speaking it into existence. One of my favorite animals is a dolphin. They are such beautiful creatures and swim through the waters so majestically. God created everything with a purpose. Yes, even mosquitoes are here for a reason. I, personally, have yet to figure out the exact reason, but I know there is one. God created the earth for us to live in while we worship Him. We are so blessed to get to live life on Earth. It is a true gift from God. There are so many beautiful sights to see here on Earth. We can see the Great Wall in China, Niagara Falls between New York and Canada, or cherry blossom season in Japan. God has given us many beautiful things to enjoy. Don't take them for granted.

Reflection

1. What is one of your favorite creations that God made?

2. Where is the most beautiful place you have been?

Day 31

Jeremiah 29:11 King James Version (KJV)

For I know the thoughts that I think toward you, saith the Lord, thoughts of peace, and not of evil, to give you an expected end.

Have you ever been told that you wouldn't amount to anything? That you weren't good enough, smart enough, etc.? Well I'm here to tell you that God has great plans for you that He knew before you were even born. He plans to carry out those plans in you if you let Him. We can stray from the path and choose not to obey what God wants us to do. But the plan that God has for you will always be there for you to pursue. His plans for you are good and you can be sure that even if it is something that scares you, He will help you do it. I never imagined that God would allow me to do public speaking or to use my social media platform to speak out but He has. Remember that God is always with us, even when we pursue things that scare us. He will be right there with you for every word you speak, every book you write, every class you teach, whatever it is He has called you to do.

Reflection:

1. Do you feel that you know your purpose?

2. If you do not feel that you know your purpose, pray and, ask God to reveal His purpose to you.

Acknowledgment

I would like to thank my mother, Kattie Douyon, for instilling a strong sense of faith in me and for raising me in church. My brother, Fisher Douyon, for always cheering me on. My cousin, Cheryl Etheredge, for always reminding me that I am capable of greatness. I would also like to thank some of my very best friends: Calan Nelson, Jessi Krauss, Amanda Gamble, Tara Carter, and Tiffany Hamm for praying for and encouraging me while I wrote this devotional. I would also like to give a special shoutout to my mentor, Michelle Conway, for love and support in writing this devotional. Also, a very special thank you to Raschelle Riley-Eaton for everything you have done for me.

Printed in the United States
By Bookmasters